extraordinary OFFICES

W
G

WATSON
GUPTILL

Author

Francisco Asensio Cerver

Editorial manager

Paco Asensio

Project coordinator

Ivan Bercedo (architect)

Graphic Design

Mireia Casanovas Soley

Layout

Òscar Lleonart Ruiz

Translation

Richard Rees

Copyediting

Michael Webb

Proofreading

Amber Ockrassa

First published in 1998 by **arco**
for Hearst Books International
1350 Avenue of the Americas
New York, NY 10019

Distributed in the U.S. and Canada by
Watson-Guptill Publications
1515 Broadway
New York, NY 10036

Distributed throughout the rest of the
world by
Hearst Books International
1350 Avenue of the Americas
New York, NY 10019

1998 © Francisco Asensio Cerver
ISBN: 0-8230-6616-9

Printed in Spain
Gráficas Iberia S.A.

BBDO WEST

Rhino Entertainment Company

Chiat/Day Advertising

@radical.media

Connors Communications

Praxair Distribution

Meyocks & Priebe Advertising

Riddell's

Ammiratis Puris Lintas

Alliance Communications Corporation

EDF-GDF Services

3 Suisses

Studio Naço

GCA Arquitectes Associats

Quatrecasas Abogados

Opportunities Centre Southall

Executive Studio

CDC Investment Management, Ltd.

Bayard Presse

Offices on Diagonal and Minerva

MEFF

Recoletos Publishers

Sony Europe Finance

Business Promotion Center

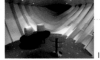

ING Bank

Long-term Credit Bank of Japan

Introduction **Offices**

Dynamism, flexibility, communication, and fluidity are words that define the offices featured in this book, as envisioned by the architects and entrepreneurs who created them. As technology has gradually freed workers from many monotonous and lonely tasks, offices are no longer exclusively the prestigious domains of managers. Instead, they are often spaces where ordinary workers create products and ideas.

In some cases, office designers themselves speak of "building an ideas and strategies factory", "a space for permanent meetings", or even "a social venue, like a cafeteria or a club." Not only do designers strive to use architecture to foster open, relaxed activity and team-oriented dialogue, they also seek to communicate through it.

An office's image is often studied with the same care as the design of a company's logo or advertising campaign. After all, the office also reflects the spirit of the company. Somewhat unsurprisingly, therefore, many of the companies whose innovative offices are presented in this book are devoted to advertising and communication, as well as to architecture.

extraordinary OFFICES

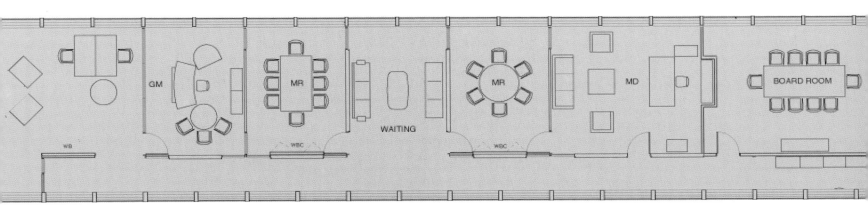

Beckson Design Associates *Interactive + Creative = ...*

The original offices were totally demolished and Three stories were reduced to two. The strategy was to create a more condensed, active, dynamic workspace. The architectural project was developed parallel to the restructuring of the company: the former hierarchical organization based on independent departments and closed offices was replaced by open spaces and flexible teams of collaborators, grouped according to clients.

In the new offices, even the president occupies a work space equal in size to those of the other employees. He explains that "in our old offices people wasted too much time in meetings. They talked a lot about what they were going to do, but they worked very little. I asked Beckson if there was a way to group people together as if they were always at a meeting. In this way communication would take place as if by osmosis, by the mere fact that they would hear and see what other people were doing."

In keeping with the new spirit of BBDO, the architects decided to create an image that would evoke not an office but an "ideas factory," adopting an industrial appearance, free of false ceilings, visible structure, and installations. In this sense, the most characteristic element is the modular system making it easy to assemble and reassemble tables and partitions. Different kinds of surfaces made from simple, cheap materials are bolted onto a meccano-type galvanized steel structure. The many awards won by the company are casually displayed at several places throughout the offices.

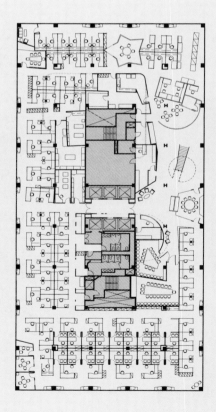

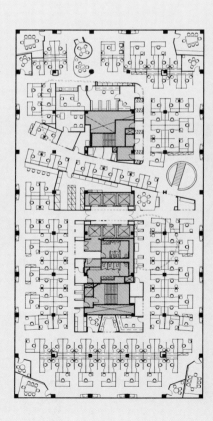

Sixteenth floor.

Seventeenth floor.

The offices provide space for over 200 employees. For this reason, the meeting areas were a crucial element in the project. In particular, the entrance hall was conceived as a multipurpose area where it is even possible to play ping-pong.

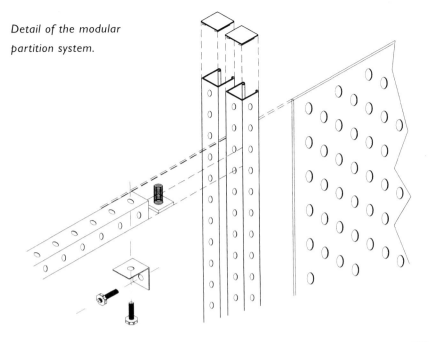

Detail of the modular partition system.

Beckson Design Associates

1985. Michael L. Beckson founds the company in Los Angeles. The present group of associates consists of Michael L. Beckson, Ed Gabor, Steven Heisler, Michael Salazar, and Laurie Meier.

Main recent works: Cinergi offices; Cook Inlet Energy Supply; Pacific Title Digital; Maverick; Soundelux; Saban Entertainment; Polygram Filmed Entertainment.

BBDO West

Address: *10960 Wilshire Boulevard, Los Angeles.*
Completed: *1995. Client: David Lubars (BBDO).*
Project: *Michael L. Beckson, Steven C. Heisler, Ed Gabor.*
Collaborators: *LaSalle Construction (general contractor); The Sheridan Group (furniture dealer); Frederick Russell Brown & Associates (mechanical/electrical engineer); Nabih Youssef & Associates (structural engineer); Cibola Systems (AV consultants).*
Photographs: *Tom Bonner.*

Beckson Design Associates

At Least We Still Have the Music

"We have created a rather unconventional environment in a conventional office building for a far from conventional company," explains Beckson. Rhino Entertainment, originally a 1970s record store, has become a constantly expanding company specializing in the promotion of music from the 1950s, 1960s and 1970s. The new head office, on Santa Monica Boulevard, occupies an area of almost 36,000 square feet in a modern office block arranged around three atria.

Despite the fact that the time frame was only sixty days, the budget around $39 per square foot, and the prevailing environment typically speculative (factors suggesting a typical layout based on partitions, straight corridors and square offices), Michael Beckson, Ed Gabor, and Steve Heisler decided to reflect the cheerful, youthful spirit of the company. The absence of a false ceiling creates the image of a warehouse or loft. The intense, random use of bright colors, both on the walls and the carpet, evokes Pop aesthetics. The corridors are full of twists and playful turns that add charm to spaces that would otherwise have been bland. The oblique planes, angular forms, and wall edges are continued on the carpet patterns, and each plane is assigned a different color, creating a composition that recalls the latest works by Sol LeWitt. Some details, such as the counters built from recycled cassette boxes, the 1960s-style furniture by Eames and Noguchi, and the placement of several palms, enhance the casual, even humorous, ambience.

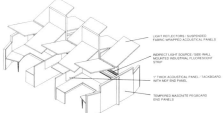

LIGHT REFLECTORS / SUSPENDED
FABRIC WRAPPED ACOUSTICAL PANELS

INDIRECT LIGHT SOURCE / SIDE-WALL
MOUNTED INDUSTRIAL FLUORESCENT
STRIP

1" THICK ACOUSTICAL PANEL / TACKBOARD
WITH MDF END PANEL

TEMPERED MASONITE PEGBOARD
END PANELS

There is no continuous false ceiling covering all the offices. Nevertheless, original acoustic ceilings have been built in some places to·help define spaces.

General plan.

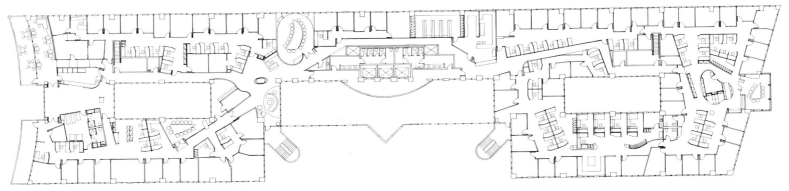

Rhino Entertainment Company

Address: *10635 Santa Monica
Boulevard, Los Angeles, CA.*
Completed: *1994.*
Client: *Rhino Entertainment
Company.*
Project: *Beckson Design Associates,
Inc. (Michael L. Beckson, Steven C.
Heisler, Edward R. Gabor).*
Collaborators: *Dinwiddie
Construction Co. (general contractor);
The Sheridan Group (furniture dealer);
Tsuchiyama & Kaino (mechanical
engineering), Dalan Engineering Inc.
(electrical engineering).*
Photographs: *Tom Bonner.*

Maybe We Should Stop

Gaetano Pesce *Calling it an "Office"*

At Chiat/Day Advertising in Manhattan, there are no private offices, not even personal tables or telephones. When employees come to the office (at different times as they have no conventional timetable and many do part of their work at home), they take what they need from a mouth-shaped counter: their computers, telephone, and files. Numerous meeting rooms are available for teamwork, as well as rooms devoted exclusively to each of the companies for which Chiat/Day Advertising work, and offices that may be reserved for an afternoon or a week.

Much of the work is done through computer networks, so these virtual meetings do not require physical space. "I believe the only way to change how people work is to put them into a completely different work environment. Throughout the whole of our lives we know where we'll sit. Now we're saying that we don't know," Jay Chiat admits.

What is the meaning of this revolution? In a world moving towards work at home, offices make sense only as a place to make a date with clients and as a space where employees can meet and communicate. Their function should not be very different from that of an employees' social club or bar, where it is possible to set up more direct relationships and greater interaction among colleagues. And its form? According to Pesce, an explosion of vibrant colors, images, graffiti, and light.

Detail of one of the
storage areas.

The flooring design
reproduces an
enormous face.

"Colors are the expression of life.
How can anyone progress in a
beige atmosphere?" says
Gaetano Pesce.

The total area of the offices is about 9,020 square feet.

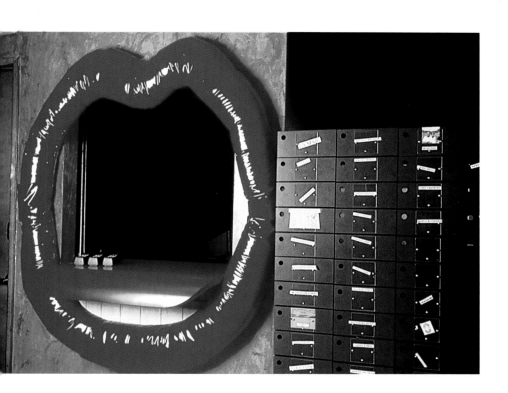

Gaetano Pesce

1939. Born in La Spezia, Italy. Graduates in architecture from the University of Venice.
1980. Moves to New York.

Main recent works: organic building in Osaka; Galerie Mourmans, Knokke-le-Zoute, Belgium; Shuman residence, New York; Torre Pluralista, Sao Paulo; installation for the entrance to the Palais des Beaux Arts, Lille.

Chiat/Day Advertising

Location: *New York.*
Completion date: *1994-1996.*
Entrepreneurs: *TBWA Chiat/Day Advertising.*
Architect: *Gaetano Pesce.*
Photographs: *Donatella Brun.*

21

Lee H. Skolnick Architecture + Design
Semi-Transparent Words

The goal of this design project was to provide a prominent New York public relations and communications firm with a variety of formal and informal meeting areas along with private and semiprivate work spaces, while creating a visually exciting and distinctive environment for interaction between staff members and clients. The variety of spaces, from private to semiprivate to common, are connected through the use of transparent and semitransparent materials to foster a sense of community, team spirit, and shared purpose. The resulting character of the space unites the potentially conflicting themes of technology, spirituality, and basic human needs.

The central space is dominantly open with shoulder-high partitions demarcating work stations. The formal conference area is defined by wood frame and glass panels that are open above to the ceiling and below to the floor. Translucent screens of wood and acrylic panels are placed at strategic sightlines, and further define the public and private areas, while maintaining the general openness and clarity of the office design. Within the structure of this basic free-form plan, the perimeter walls remain mostly white, whereas specific service areas are highlighted by the use of colors.

Architectural elements such as the closet, the production room door, and the curved kitchen wall are distinguished by the use of stained plywood, contrasting the lighter tones of all other furnishings. Wood is the primary material, providing continuity and warmth: the storage cabinetry and closets for client's products are in birch, and mahogany underlines some desks and wall panels. Accent materials used include aluminum wall, Formica (for durability in service areas), natural maple wood caps and galvanized steel trim (for the cubicles' partitions); and custom-made fiberglass shoji screens.

Wood is the predominant material in the offices: flooring, vertical partitions, furniture. It creates a sensation of continuity and great warmth. The shelves are of beech. Strips of mahogany offset the counters and some of the panels.

Ground plan.

1. Entrance.
2. Reception and waiting area.
3. Conference room.
4. President's office.
5. Operations room.
6. Open offices area.
7. Production room.
8. Lavatories.
9. Kitchen.
10. Meeting and rest area.

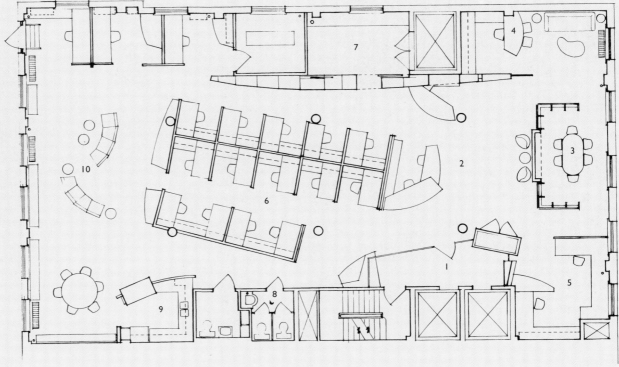

Although closed by no doors, the kitchen is concealed behind a green plywood panel.

Aspect of the meeting room, separated from the rest of the office by a wood and glass structure.

Lee H. Skolnick

1979. Graduates as an architect from Cooper Union, New York.
1980. Founds L.H. Skolnick Architecture + Design.

Paul Alter

1982. Graduates as an architect from Cooper Union, New York.
1982-1986. Works at Davis, Brody and Associates.
1986. Joins L.H. Skolnick Architecture + Design.

Main works: Mohonk Preserve head offices, New York; Creative Discovery Museum, Chattanooga; Enchanted Planet Restaurant, New York; Scholastic Galleries, New York; Western Heritage Museum, Omaha; Marine Park Environmental Education Center, Brooklyn.

Connors Communications

Address: *30 West 21st Street, New York, USA.*
Completion date: *1995.*
Client: *CONNORS COMMUNICATIONS/Connie Connors.*
Cost: *$322,000*
Project: *Lee H. Skolnick, Paul Alter.*
Collaborators: *Margaret García (project architect).*
Photographs: *Andrew Garn.*

27

The Media also Has a Little Heart

Rockwell Group

Above the entrance door, on a sign that seems to have been recovered from an old 19th-century warehouse, we see the name of the company, "@radical.media", and underneath, "never established." This little joke throws light on the attitudes and image this multimedia company wishes to project. President Jon Kamen chose the loft of an industrial building on the edge of Manhattan for his new offices. He wanted a space as open as possible to foster communication between the members of a dynamic, flexible, egalitarian team. To this end, he got in touch with David Rockwell, whom he had known since he built his own home ten years earlier and whose practice he considered eminently capable of developing theme architecture. Rockwell's idea was for a space characterized by industrial finishes, looking rather like a 1950s warehouse. The structure of large, open rooms has been preserved, the different work places being limited by half-height partitions made from plywood panels.

The ceilings are unfaced, leaving the electrical wiring and air-conditioning installation in full view. The flooring is a continuous slab of concrete. The few divisions consist of glass doors that echo the existing windows of the old warehouse. The shelves are recycled galvanized steel scaffolding, while the boardroom table is a tubular structure on castors. Finally, most of the furniture has been recovered from the 1950s.

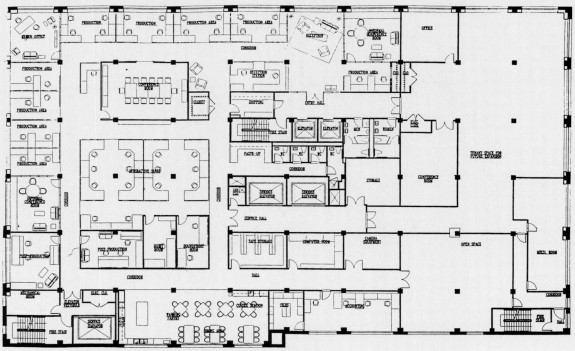

The sliding sheet-metal door leading into the boardroom has been recovered from an old warehouse.

The conference room looks like a film set.

Two easy chairs, a sofa, a few small tables, and a vase of flowers: the reception area is conceived as an improvised waiting room.

The kitchen-break room is one of
the most important parts of the
office space, conceived as an
informal meeting place for the
team members. It is almost like a
domestic kitchen in appearance.

David Rockwell

1956. Born in Chicago. Graduated as an architect from Syracuse University.

Rockwell Group

Main recent works: Planet Hollywood restaurants all over the world; Official All Star Café restaurants all over the US; Monkey, Torre de Pisa, Charley O's restaurants, New York; Morgenthal Frederics Opticians on Madison Ave., New York; Cosmetics Plus stores, New York; CBS store, New York.

@radical.media

Address: *435 Hudson Street, New York.*
Completion date: *1996.*
Client: *Jon Kamen (@radical.media)*
Project: *Rockwell Group.*
Collaborators: *Silver Rail Construction Corporation (general contractor); Electrical Systems Engineering (electrical consultants); T.A.s. Engineering (mechanical consultants); Focus Lighting (lighting).*
Photographs: *Paul Warchol.*

Herbert Lewis Kruse Blunck Architecture

Giving Underrated Materials their Due

An existing 58,000-square-foot warehouse, within an industrial park, was modified to house a distribution and processing center for welding supplies. One third of the facility was converted to house the office, conference, and training operations. Two thirds of the facility remained as a warehouse. The industrial nature of the operation was expressed by leaving the shell and structure of the building exposed throughout the entire facility. The interdependence of both the warehouse and office operations was reinforced by this common expression.

The warehouse shelving system was used to create the structure and framework for the office mezzanine area. Windows could not be added to existing precast panels, so daylight was introduced by adding skylights, which backlit a wall of translucent fiberglass and distributed the light throughout the office area. The wall also screened existing major utility connections so they would not have to be moved. Conference and training areas were located by the existing windows near the entry.

All systems, including mechanical, electrical, office structure, and furnishings, were based on a clear, linear organization to allow for orderly, systematic expansion. The addition of a parking lot along with an extension of the exterior entry areas and landscaping are currently under construction. The creation of an effective and efficient layout with an identity appropriate to the owner's operation, and a budget consistent with warehouse development, were the primary goals guiding the project.

Ground floor.

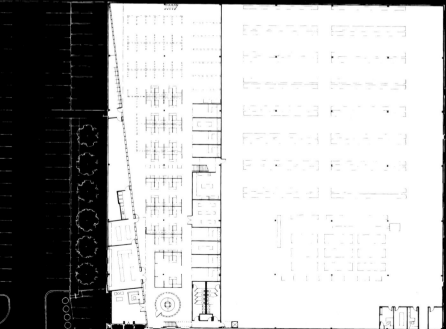

The undulating fiberglass wall separates the meeting and training areas from the rest of the offices.

The air-conditioning shafts are used as compositional elements.

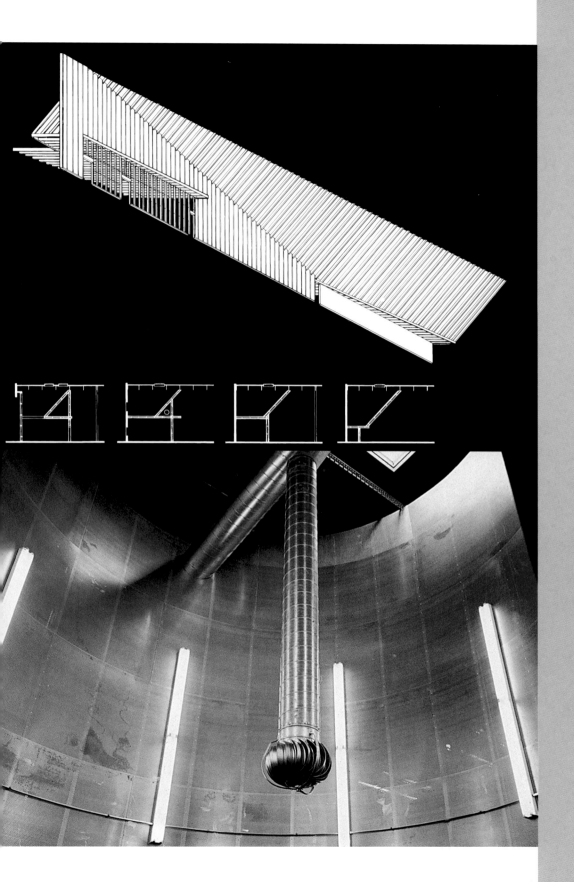

Herbert Lewis Kruse Blunck Architecture

1961. Charles Herbert & Associates is founded.
1987. Herbert Lewis Kruse Blunck Architecture founded as a continuation of Charles Herbert & Associates. The main partners are Charles Herbert, Calvin Lewis, Rod Kruse and Kirk von Blunck.

Main recent works: Hub Tower/Kaleidoscope shopping and office complex, Des Moines; Valley National Bank restoration, Des Moines; Des Moines Civic Center; Meredith Corporation offices, Des Moines.

Praxair Distribution, Inc.

Location: *Ankeny, Iowa, USA.*
Completion Date: *1997.*
Client: *Praxair, Inc.*
Project: *Herbert Lewis Kruse Blunck Architecture.*
Collaborators: *Neumann Brothers Construction (general contractor); Charles Saul Engineering (structural engineer); Stroh Corporation (electrical/mechanical sub-contractor).*
Photographs: *Farshid Assassi.*

Herbert Lewis Kruse Blunck Architecture

A Granary in the Office

This Midwestern advertising agency's client base is comprised almost exclusively of advertisers specializing in the field of agribusiness. A scheme that makes distinct references to the effects of the Midwest's farm economy was, from the onset, an obvious thematic choice. Working from a general plan that formalized the agency's functional requirements, the 14,500-square-foot lease space, and modest budget, the architect and the client began a directed but admittedly intuitive investigation of Iowa's farm vernacular.

Typical regional construction practices were observed and recorded; common farm building materials were documented along with their use, finish, and means of attachment. The designers pored over standard references on rural construction as well as catalogs of farm implements, machinery, hardware, and agricultural supplies. Out of this investigation, instinctive reinterpretations of local farm imagery were selectively adapted to various uses throughout the lease space.

Corrugated metal grain bins, the most literal of the designers' interpretations, become meeting areas for the agency's staff and outside vendors. Raw, stud-framed walls, variously clad in unfinished plywood, translucent fiberglass sheathing, and sheets of perforated metal panel enclose common work areas, paste-up rooms, and office space for the agency designers responsible for the creative inception of the firm's advertising campaigns. For the centrally located boardroom, the scale and atmosphere of a lowly Iowa corncrib is convincingly recreated. Subdued, external light hazily drifts through the room's humbly rendered, slat-wall enclosure. Paired sidewall studs extend upward, engaging stoutly-anchored crossbracing and undressed stud rafters. Even the room's wide glass and corrugated metal conference table picks up the thematic flavor.

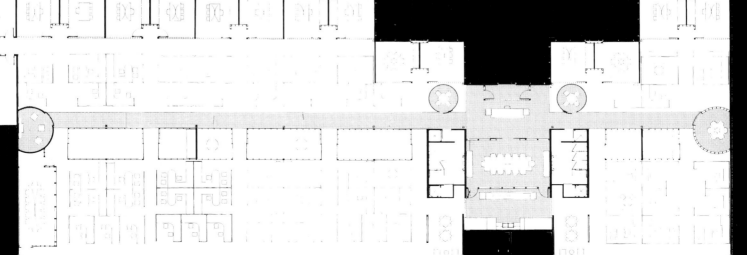

Ground plan.

From the axonometric we appreciate the fact that the offices are arranged like a complex of independent rural constructions.

Meyocks & Priebe Advertising, Inc.

Location: *Des Moines, Iowa, USA.*
Completion Date: *1996.*
Client: *Meyocks & Priebe Advertising, Inc.*
Project: *Herbert Lewis Kruse Blunck Architecture.*
Collaborators: *Taylor Ball (general contractor); Charles Saul Engineering (structural engineer); Baker Mechanical (mechanical sub-contractor); ABC Electrical, Inc. (electrical sub-contractor).*
Photographs: *Farshid Assassi.*

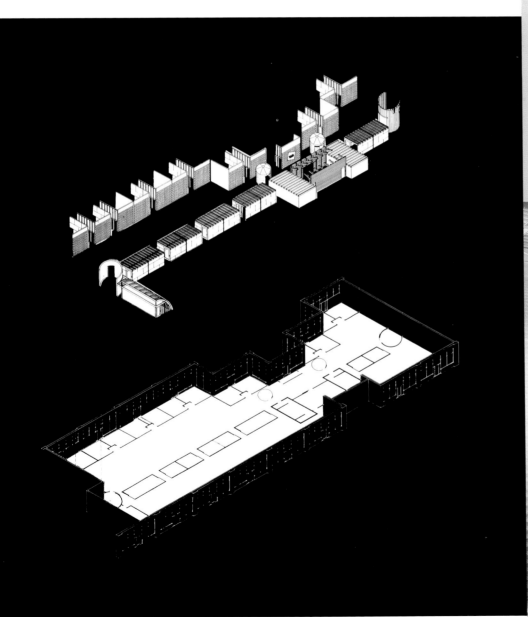

William P. Bruder | *Little by Little, a Tree*

This three-story office building, built for a Jackson Hole ad agency, can be found in the new business district, in an area where development has not spoiled the natural beauty of the surroundings. The triple height atrium is illuminated by a long, narrow ascending window that folds over and turns into a skylight when it reaches the ceiling. This empty space forms the project's center, and the offices are organized around it.

Wood is the project's main architectural theme, articulating the spatial dimensions and at the same time organizing and shaping how the building is likely to be interpreted. Wood is presented on a large and small scale, and contributes to the overall structure as well as to the details, and evokes the culture of the craftsman.

In the interior, in Bruder's own words, there is a dialogue between space, light, and wood. The visitor or client reaches the reception after crossing a concrete ramp, guided by an access canopy consisting of three horizontal tree trunks over the entrance. The reception itself consists of a round counter between two tree trunks supporting the roof. All of this is within the center of a triple height, vertical space that is bathed in light. Here, also, is a hydraulic elevator and a gentle-edged, Japanese-style garden with bamboo and three large, randomly-placed stones. On the second and third floors, the offices of the accounting and design departments are private. The panoramic views of the mountains enjoyed from these offices tend to dilute the impact of the surrounding city.

A library and a large conference room, designed for product presentation, have been located in the balconies which overlook the hall.

Sections.

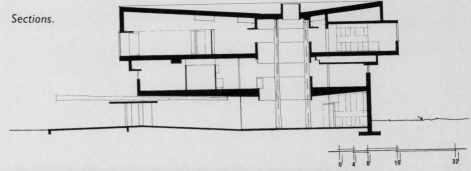

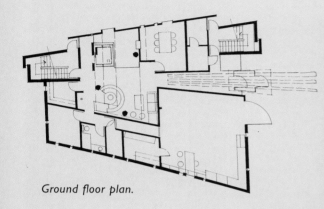

Ground floor plan.

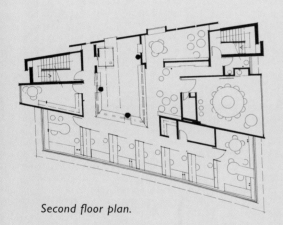

Second floor plan.

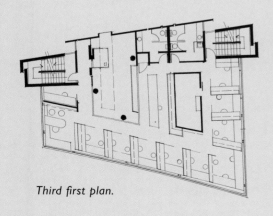

Third first plan.

William P. Bruder

1946. Born in Milwaukee, Wisconsin.
1969. Graduates as a sculptor from the University of Wisconsin.
1969-1974. Works at Gunner Birkerts Associate Architects.
1974. Sets up his own studio in Phoenix, Arizona.

Main works, 1990-1997:
Hill/Shepard House; Kol Ami Temple; Riddell's offices, Wyoming; Phoenix Central Library; Scottsdale Museum of Contemporary Art.

Riddell's

Location: *Jackson Hole, Wyoming*
Date of Construction: *1995.*
Promoter: *Riddell's Advertising and Design Agency.*
Architect: *William P. Bruder.*
Collaborators: *Ed Ewers, Dewayne Smyth, and Maryann Bloomfield (design team).*
Photographs: *Bill Timmerman.*

Kuwabara Payne McKenna Blumberg Architects *Simplicity*

The Ammirati Puris Lintas offices express the agency's philosophy within the framework of a carefully crafted architectural style which results in an understated and functional workplace. The design creates a clean, light, and uncluttered interior to serve a range of creative, accounting, and research activities. The style emphasizes the creative vitality of the agency's workers.

The design concept emphasizes visual and spatial connectedness to the urban culture of Manhattan. Several views, including those of the East River and the United Nations Headquarters, cap off the reception area and the main circulation routes through the office. The city's grid of streets and parks serves as the controlling metaphor for the floor plan.

A well-defined sequence of spaces, beginning with the entrance and flowing into the reception, conference, and work areas, organizes the plan into patterns of movement and open areas. Within this order, a series of prototypical modules for executive offices, standard offices, open workstations, and staff assistant stations create integrated work areas to reinforce a spirit of collaboration and teamwork.

The typical characteristics of the New York loft: white walls, high ceilings, natural lighting, and abundant open space: are reflected in the design of the office interior. The materials and color palette used are limited to white paint for walls, columns, and ceilings; gray carpeting for floors; and hardwood flooring at selected reception and client waiting areas. Custom-designed elements in beech wood, white Carrara marble tops, and perforated metal, impart a sense of richness and texture to the disciplined work environment.

The different working areas are separated by partitions which do not reach the ceiling.

The project involved the renovation of 14 floors of an office block built in 1970. The total surface area is around 210,000 sq.ft. The project cost 20 million dollars.

Plan of floor 38.

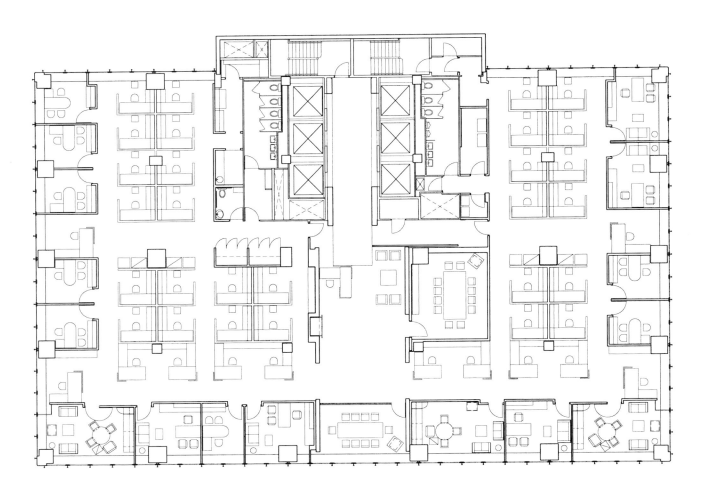

View of one of the reception
areas.

The longitude of these spaces
allows the superpositioning
of different planes. The photos on
this page show how, although
there is no visual separation,
the waiting and resting
areas are clearly differentiated.

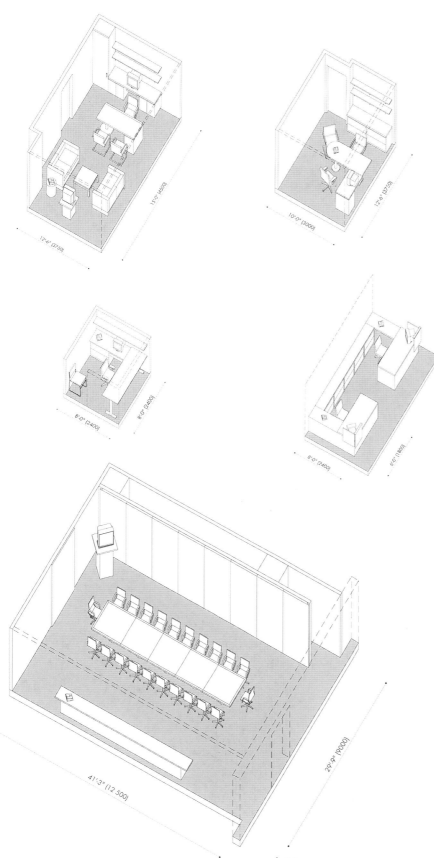

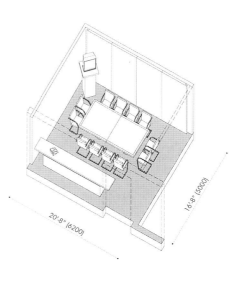

15'-0" (4500)

12'-6" (3750)

10'-0" (3000)

12'-6" (3750)

8'-0" (2400)

8'-0" (2400)

8'-0" (2400)

6'-0" (1800)

41'-3" (12 500)

29'-9" (9000)

20'-8" (6200)

16'-8" (5000)

Kuwabara Payne McKenna Blumberg Architects

1987. Bruce Kuwabara, Thomas Payne, Marianne McKenna and Shirley Blumberg start their architectural firm in Toronto. All had previously worked for Barton Myers Associates from the last years of the seventies until 1987.

Main works between 1990-1998: Woodsworth College, Toronto. Kitchener City Hall, Toronto. Joseph S.Stauffer Library, Kingston. Offices for Ammirati Puris Lintas, New York. Disney Television Studios, Toronto. Shops for Crabtree & Evelyn and Indigo Books.

Ammiratis Puris Lintas

Location: *One Dag Hammarskjold Plaza, Manhattan, New York.*
Inauguration Date: *1996.*
Client: *Ammiratis Puris Lintas.*
Architects: *Bruce Kuwabara, Shirley Blumberg, Kevin Mast, David Jesson.*
Associates: *John Frondisi (local architect); Structure Tone (contractor).*
Photography: *ESTO.*

Kuwabara Payne Mckenna Blumberg Architects *Foregrounds*

Alliance Communications Corporation, a leading Canadian film distribution and production company, selected Kuwabara Payne McKenna Blumberg Architects in an invitation-only design competition for its new head offices in Toronto. In order to meet the requirements of the client's budget, the design strategy is focused on the creative link between the three levels of the companies offices, and reinforcing, through the architecture, the Alliance's identity as a leading force in the national film industry.

A thick, cherrywood-clad wall represents the major feature in the scheme. It creates a conceptual north-south axis that organizes the overall spatial plan to create visual connections with the downtown area to the south and the green landscape of Rosedale, a residential area, to the immediate north. The wall rises through three stories of the office tower and forms a backdrop for orientation and reception.

A generous opening carved from the slab permits views through the three levels and is intersected by a steel and stone stairway. The stairs facilitate internal circulation and ascend along the wall. The elevator lobbies of the 15th and 16th floors are distinguished by a cleft-faced slate wall that visually lead visitors into the reception areas. On the 14th floor, a translucent acrylic and aluminum-framed screen separates the public areas from internal staff work spaces. Custom-designed frames for movie posters highlight the company's identity.

Although the building's existing stairs and elevators could have been used, it was considered necessary to build private staircases to ensure good communication between the different departments.

Floor 16.

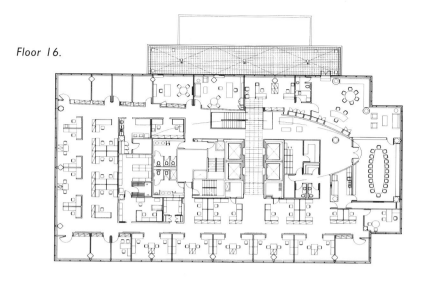

Floor 15.

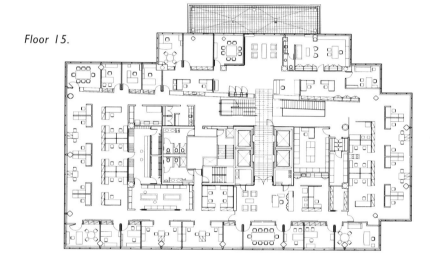

Floor 14.

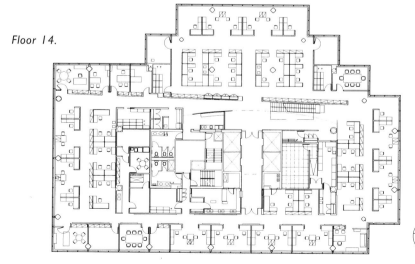

Alliance Communications Corporation

Location: *121 Bloor Street East, Toronto, Ontario, Canada.*
Completion Date: *1996.*
Client: *Alliance Communications Corporation.*
Project: *Shirley Blumberg (partner-in-charge); Bruce Kuwabara (partner, design); Karen Cvornyek, David Polloway (senior project architects); Andrew Dyke, Marco Magarelli.*
Consultants: *Read Jones Christoffersen (structural); Mulvey & Banani International (electrical); Smith & Anderson (mechanical); Suzanne Powadiuk (lighting); Valcoustics (acoustics).*
Photographs: *Robert Burley.*

Chance Encounters in
Quatre Plus *Unlikely Places*

The most interesting aspect of this project in the high-rise La Défense district of Paris is the treatment of collective spaces, the waiting areas, and the corridors. In Quatre Plus' project these often insipid and neglected elements become genuine centers of communication between different company teams, often used as alternative, informal conference rooms where management runs more smoothly and problems are solved more easily.

These spaces lack natural light, so curved, vibrantly colored partitions with capricious angles are combined with glass screens to create a dynamic environment and prevent any feeling of claustrophobia. In high-traffic areas, walls are articulated or revolve around the pillars. The floating parquet floor provides a warmth rarely found in office buildings.

The bar treatment is paradigmatic, since the architects consider it one of the most important elements in the building. The lavatories and appliances that normally occupy office corridors (photocopy and vending machines, reception counters, and so on) here become strange, colorful artifacts, playful and even ironic. In their presence, we invariably recall the universe of Sottsass. Quatre Plus uses these pieces to introduce oblique lines and unexpected directrices to destructure what would otherwise be an excessively orthogonal and rigid space.

Waiting and rest areas.

View of one of the reception and correspondence counters.

View of the bar.

The offices have been conceived taking into account ergonomic factors relative to the visual and acoustical environments and the quality of the air.

The compositional criterion applied to the corridors is extended into the offices.

Fourth floor plan.

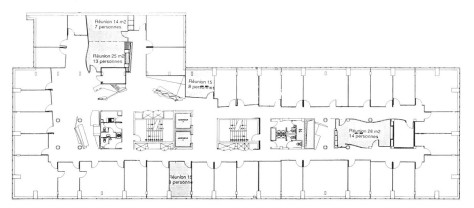

Quatre Plus

1987. Gilles Gary, Paul Achard, Bruno Michel and Pierre Virnot found Quatre Plus in Paris.

Main recent works:
Scetauroute offices in Saint-Quentin-en-Yvelines; Ponts et Chaussées central laboratories, Bougenais; water research center, Antony; France Telecom, Bobigny; Rennes management center; CIG, examination and competitions center.

EDF-GDF Services

Location: *La Défense, Paris, France.*
Completion Date: *1994.*
Client: *Électricité de France - Gaz de France.*
Project: *Quatre Plus (Gilles Gary, Paul Achard, Bruno Michel, Pierre Virnot).*
Photographs: *Luc Boegly.*

Studio Naço | *The Digital City*

The Cité Numérique is the new head office of 3 Suisses, one of the most important sale-by-catalog companies in France. This building, with an area of almost 26,250 square feet, is given over entirely to the creation and generation of new images, either to be printed on paper or diffused in multimedia format or via the Internet. The offices are occupied by artistic directors, photographers, graphic designers, a whole gamut of high-tech equipment, virtual decors, and image banks. The camera on any of the sets is connected by network to the screen of the graphic designer working on the catalog, making possible simultaneous teamwork even though the photographer may be 500 kilometers away.

The kind of relationships established between employees, links to technology, and data transmission by means very different from the traditional all have undoubtable repercussions on the way space is occupied. Consequently, Studio Naço had to rethink their work as architects to develop this project. In this sense, their strategy is closer to that of image producers (such as the creative professionals employed by 3 Suisses) than to that of builders who are constrained by regulations and typologies.

Alain Renk and Marcelo Joulia strive to arouse an emotional reaction in those who use their architecture; to create sensations through original spatial projects and unusual forms. The surprise, the visual effect, or the anecdote are not whims on the part of the architects but rather a way to ensure that spaces will have a face and an identity, allowing both employees and visitors to establish an affectionate relationship with them.

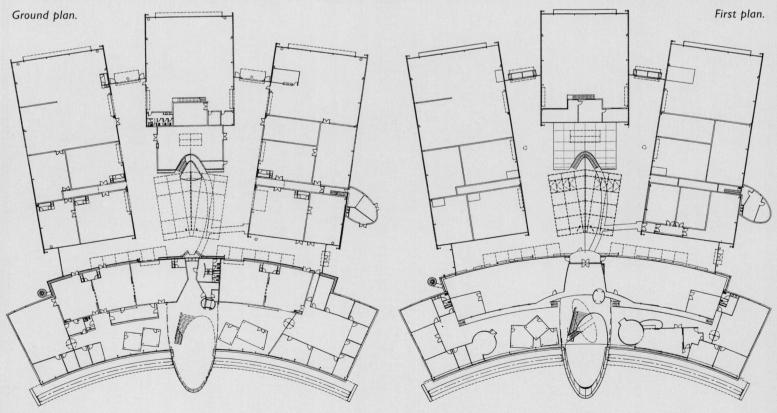

Ground plan.   *First plan.*

Studio Naço

1986. Alain Renck and Marcelo Joulia found Studio Naço in Paris.

Main recent works: Tacoma record store, Nantes; Conseil Général de Belfort; alterations to the Montreuil city hall; Who's the Next fashion agency, Paris; Gagnaire Restaurant, Saint-Étienne; Studio Naço head offices, Paris.

La Cité Numérique

Location: *Villeneuve-d'Ascq, France.*
Completion date: *1994.*
Client: *3 Suisses.*
Architects: *Studio Naço (Alain Renk, Marcelo Joulia).*
Collaborators: *Jean-François Pasqualini, Allard Kuyken, Beatrice Berián (architects); Muriel Quintanilla (designer); Olivier Dubos (graphic design).*
Photographs: *Mario Pignata-Monti.*

Where the Wood Used to Be

Studio Naço

The Naço offices are located in a block interior in the Paris quarter of La Bastille. Alain Renk and Marcelo Joulia decided to rehabilitate an old, lumber warehouse on Boulevard Diderot and convert it into their headquarters. The first operation consisted of demolishing the garage that occupied the ground floor and concealed the warehouse from view, and of converting it into an entrance patio; the second operation, of removing the existing facade and revealing the spectacular old wooden structure of the warehouse; and the third, of enveloping the building in a transparent steel and glass skin and installing an electronic system by which to open and close the windows. The result is a work of extraordinary impact.

The old warehouse is sectioned to display the office layout. From the patio, and through the glazed facade, it is possible to observe the designers and architects as they work in apparent silence. The three floors of around 390 square feet each constitute completely open, naked spaces. A closed box, christened la boîte, contains the services on each floor (lavatories, wardrobe, and building services on the ground floor; photocopy machine and archives on the second; fax and storage area on the third).

In the interiors a contrast is established between the structure and the furniture. The whole structure, joists and pillars in aged wood, the rubble stone walls and the stone flooring, is left visible, and Naço occupies this cherished space not only with their presence but also with their designs, the furniture that they themselves have created, such as lamps and radios. Their ingenious and colorful products endow the austere, old, lumber warehouse with life.

Previous page: two moments in the dismantling process of the former warehouse facade.

Above: Nighttime view of the definitive glass facade.

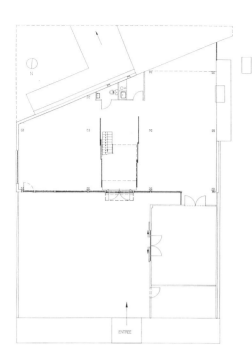

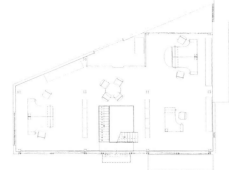

The ground floor, with
the adjacent patio and
workshop.

Second floor.

Third floor.

Naço work at two opposite
extremes: the structure and
the furniture. Partitions,
doors, and false ceilings are
excluded from the project.

Section.

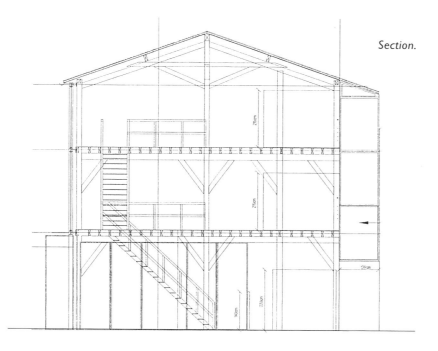

Studio Naço

Address: _66, Bd. Diderot, Paris, France._
Completion date: _1994._
Client: _Studio Naço._
Architects: _Studio Naço (Alain Renk, Marcelo Joulia)._
Collaborators: _Jean-François Pasqualini, Allard Kuyken, Beatrice Berián (architects); Muriel Quintanilla (designer); Olivier Dubos (graphics)._
Photographs: _Mario Pignata-Monti._

GCA Arquitectes Associats | *1:1 Model and We Carry On Working*

The studio of the GCA team of architects is immersed in the homogeneous urban tissue of Barcelona, occupying former textile warehouses on the ground floor of a 1946 building. Within the textile tradition it was common practice to place the offices at the front, beneath the rest of the building, while the whole of the rear part would be occupied by the warehouses. The fact that the building followed these criteria was crucial to the project. Typically, offices were located beside the entry, with cornices, moldings, and compartmentalized spaces; meanwhile, the interior consisted of an empty space supported by metal profiles consisting of bases and riveted shafts.

Here, the architects opted for a twofold strategy: on one hand, they preserved the appearance of the existing offices by restoring the carpentry and adding installations to create the reception, administration and work control areas; on the other, they created a clearly modern space devoted to design in the former warehouse. The project is based on a dialogue between opposites. Nevertheless, the space given over to design becomes virtually the absolute protagonist of the offices. It was conceived as a large white box lit from above by two huge skylights inside which an itinerary is established (projects and drawing room, project management office and so on) that reflects the gestation process of work.

This sequence of spaces ends at a large exterior patio. Light is the primordial element here. White walls, maple flooring, and glass partitions together configure a neutral, homogeneous, minimalist space in which spatial limits disappear and multiple views and perspectives are established.

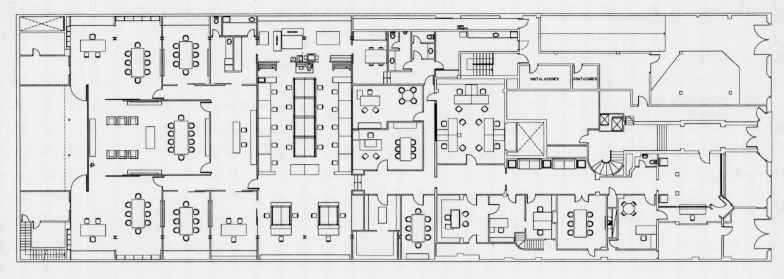

General ground plan.

Longitudinal section.

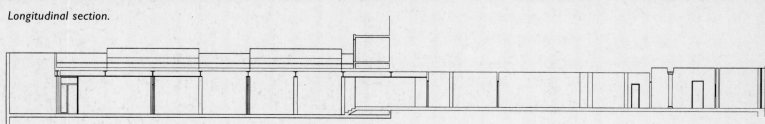

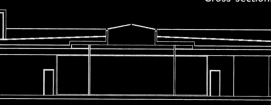

Cross section.

The furniture was conceived according to a single design criterion to minimize the use of materials and obtain a compact image with practically no color variation.

GCA Arquitectes Associats

1986. Josep Juanpere (1952, Barcelona) and Antoni Puig (1958, Barcelona) found GCA. Associated architects are Josep Riu, Jesús Hernando, and Arturo de la Maza.

Main recent works: Paco and Paco Rabanne stores in Paris; Pronovias factory and offices, Barcelona; Hotel Condes, Barcelona; Hotel Havana, Barcelona; Quatrecasas offices, Barcelona and Madrid; Hotel Santo Mauro, Madrid.

Oficinas de GCA Arquitectes Associats

Address: *Valencia 289, Barcelona, Spain.*
Completion date: *1996*
Client: *GCA*
Project: *Josep Juanpere, Antoni Puig, Josep Riu, Jesús Hernando and Arturo de la Maza*
Collaborators: *CODESCA (general contractor); Gerelec (electricity and lighting); Ebanistería Pomar (carpentry); CLIMATERM (heating and air conditioning)*
Photographs: *Jordi Miralles*

The offices benefit from two skylights that originally belonged to the textile warehouses.

GCA Arquitectes Associats *Legitimate defense*

GCA Arquitectes Associats were commissioned to organize the work space of the offices of the legal firm of Quatrecasas. The space consisted of three floors at the base of the building for housing the law offices and three floors in the tower for other services.

The central feature of the design is the patio, which was converted from an outside space to an inside one in order to vertically integrate the various floors and to make the essential spatial unity of the complex more apparent. This conversion was achieved by building a transparent dome and a new staircase, consisting of steps of green marble supported by stainless steel struts.

The patio extends three floors and is covered by a glass skylight. The stairway, made of glass and steel and suspended from a hanging structure, is visually prominent. The feeling of transparency and lightness that it provides is enhanced by the curtain-wall of glass supported by steel ties and clamps on one side, with the other sides made of conventional glass.

The stairway, dome, and curtain-wall of the patio are finished with painted steel and stainless steel structures, all of which serve as a counterpoint to the other materials used in the design of the offices.

To impart a unique corporate image to the firm, GCA Arquitectes Associats have tried to create an atmosphere of seriousness and practicality while at the same time creating a sense of modernity and technological sophistication. The decision of the designers to use only natural materials, such as marble, cherry wood, and leather upholstery, also contributes to this sense of seriousness and sophistication.

The designers have chosen
to use only noble materials
marble, cherrywood and
leather upholstery.
The lighting of the waiting
rooms is tenuous and diffuse
and creates a comfortable
atmosphere.

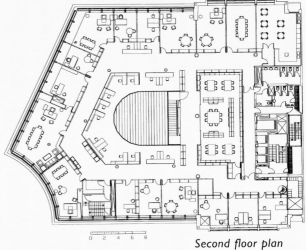

Second floor plan

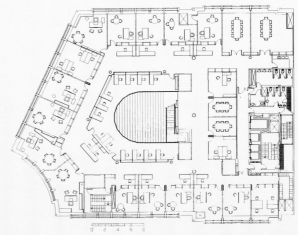

Third floor plan

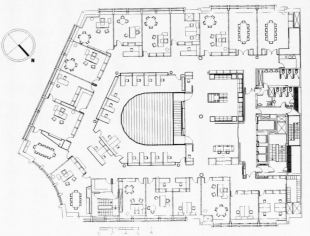

Fourth floor plan

The offices occupy three floors of the building. The central space is a huge patio which extends for three floors, covered by a glass skylight. In the space, the stair way, made of glass and steel and suspended from a hanging structure, plays a central role.

Quatrecasas Abogados

Location: *Passeig de Gràcia, Barcelona.*
Inauguration date: *1997.*
Client: *Quatrecasas Abogados.*
Design: *GCA Arquitectes Associats.*
Associates: *J. Tressera and Mateo Grassi (Furniture design), XEDED (carpentry), Òscar Tusquets (seating), ARLEX (screens).*
Photography: *Lluís Casals.*

The Strategy of
Studio Downie | *Opportunity*

As part of its strategy to improve training and enterprise opportunities for local people, West London Training & Enterprise Council (TEC) envisaged a series of Opportunities Centers, or 'one-stop shops' containing support activities to provide access to employment, training and business development opportunities in High Street. The first Opportunities Center is located in the heart of the community in the former Southall Town Hall, unused for several years but part of London's vibrant Asian community.

The building had a fine classical elevation and important presence within the local townscape, but internally was a maze of dark, unattractive, and confusing corridors and rooms. The brief from West London TEC's Chief Executive, Dr. Phil Blackburn, was to create an open, welcoming, and simple interior. Studio Downie's approach was to remove all ground floor walls to form a single, open 'chessboard' upon which were placed a series of objects separating space into large and small, public and private. The primary installation is a long 'information wall' containing libraries, public information, computer screens, and the reception desk.

To the front are the public spaces and behind the interview and office spaces. A management development center is located on the upper floor, offering courses for individuals and small businesses. Natural MDF and wood is used in the public areas for the information wall and ceilings, respectively, to provide an ambience warmer than that normally associated with commercial interiors. This is countered with a single, strong, vibrant color.

The hall, next to the reception counter, is covered by white cotton canvas held in position by guy wires. In the words of Craig Downie, it is a symbol of peace and hope.

A series of very simple elements transforms the exterior image of the facade: a thin aluminum canopy, glass doors, and dramatic lighting.

1. Entrance.
2. Reception.
3. Interview room.
4. Lavatories.
5. Elevator.
6. Fire station.
7. Office.

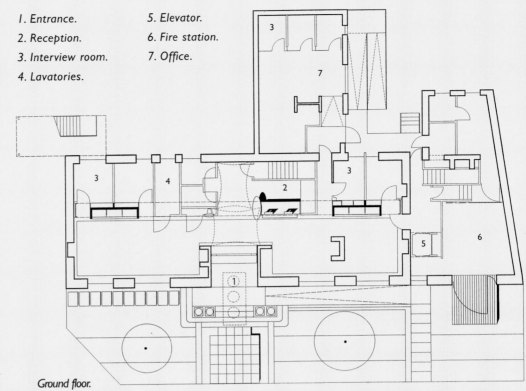

Ground floor.

Ground-floor axonometric.

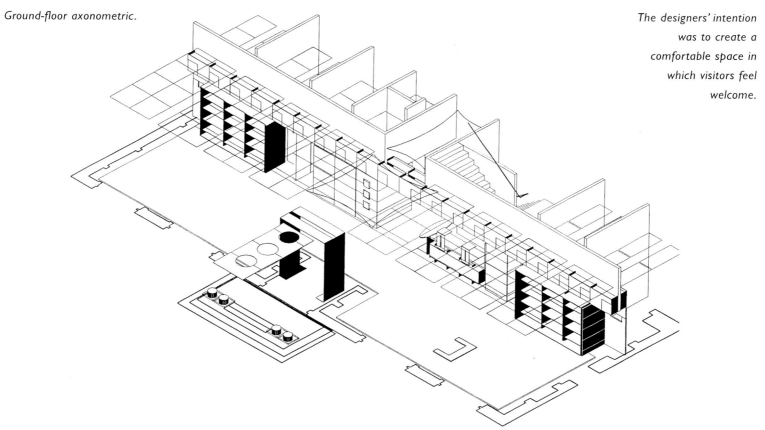

Section of the entrance. The ceiling is covered by a series of stretched canvases.

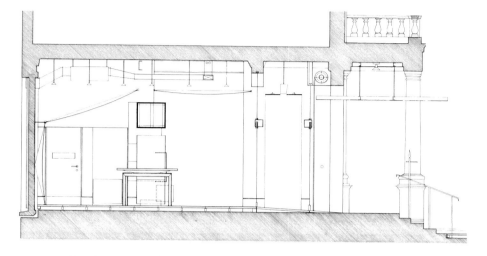

Studio Downie Architects

1992. Craig Downie founds his own company after having worked for Terry Farrell Partnership and Foster Associates.
1993. Enters into a partnership with Andrew Jackson.

Main recent works: Treasury Offices, France; private lake house in California; Remodeling of a square in Sheffield; art galleries in France and London. Craig Downie also acted as consultant in the design of Heathrow Airport interiors.

Opportunities Center

Location: *Southall, West London, UK.*
Completion Date: *1996.*
Client: *West London Training & Enterprise Council.*
Project: *Craig Downie, Andrew Jackson, Arita Patel, Chris Harrison, Laura Downie.*
Collaborators: *Gilby Construction (general contractor); Durley Hill (structural engineer); Brinkfell Partnership (electrical/mechanical); Davis Langdon & Everest (quantity surveyor).*
Photographs: *Peter Cook/VIEW.*

Words Suspended in

Studio Downie

the Half-Darkness

The vision for The Executive Studio came from research in 1992 by the Training & Enterprise Council (TEC) into how information technology is used in business. The findings showed that there were large gaps in the public's understanding of how best to use technology and how to maximize its use to make their business successful. Businesses also needed a facility where they could experience technology in a practical environment. To meet those needs, the Studio was created. Its mission is to help organizations manage information to transform business performance and sharpen their competitive edge.

The architects' challenge was to create an environment that challenged the perception of corporate spaces placed within a traditional floor plan. Three bold interrelated spaces, each with its own colored wall, were created. The demonstration suite, a long, rectangle extruded from the existing fabric, is the heart of the Studio. Visitors enter the departure lounge to log-in, relax, and use games and Internet resources. From here they step into the flexible demonstration suite where software and applications are tested. This provides a platform for software demonstrations, exhibits, seminars, lectures, and receptions.

The Office of the Future and Learning Center are located at each end, and can be opened up to the main space. Materials are mainly aluminum, glass, and polycarbonate with opaque graphics. The boardroom is an interactive software-inspired, 20-place, glass circular table with concealed computers, also designed by Studio Downie Architects. A central silver ceiling cone conceals four projectors. The ambience of the spaces is of calm and simplicity with a computerized, constantly changing spectrum of color.

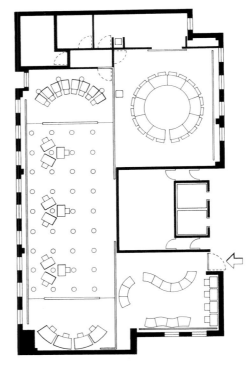

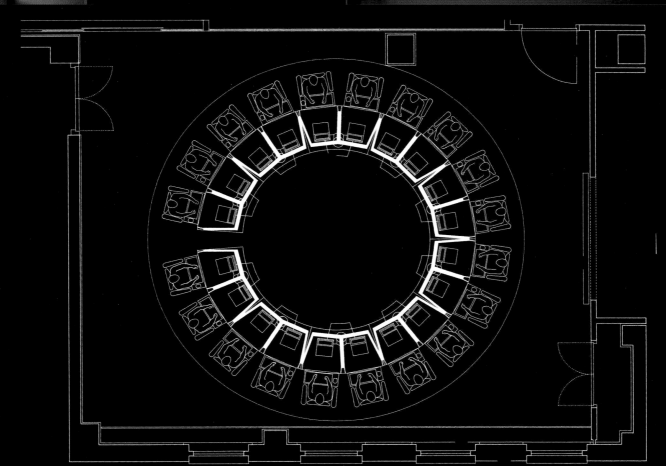

In the darkness of the offices, the signs designating the various rooms mingle with the texts on the computer screens.

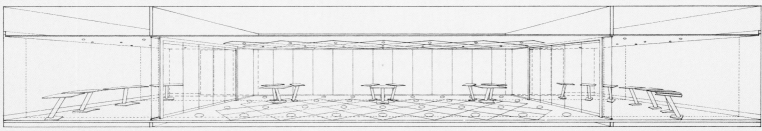

View of the boardroom. On the ceiling, a an aluminium cone contains four projectors.

The circular table was designed by the Studio Downie Architects. The top is glass. The computer screen is below, seen through the glass top.

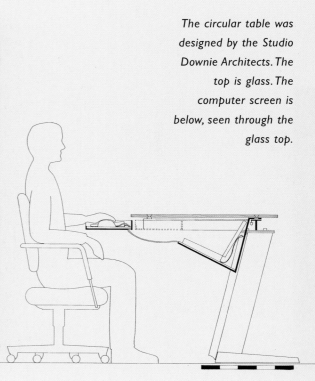

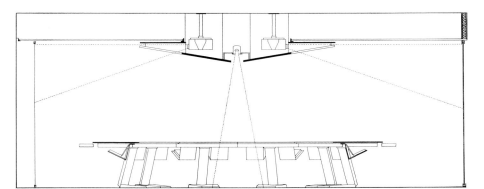

The Executive Studio

Location: *West London Center,*
Hounslow, West London, UK.
Completion Date: *1997.*
Client: *West London Training &*
Enterprise Council.
Project: *Craig Downie, Andrew*
Jackson, David Hanna, Chris
Binsted.
Collaborators: *Dewhurst*
MacFarlane (structural engineer);
Davis Langdon & Everest (quantity
surveyor).
Photographs: *Chris*
Gascoigne/VIEW.

Downie Studio | **Money curves**

The client, the investment section of the Caisse de Dépôts, a part of the French Treasury, needed new offices and space for meetings and conferences in an center of London. They chose an existing building in an area near Piccadilly.

The commission was to design four offices, meeting rooms, a hall, reception area, and an administration area with space for four people. One of the main requirements was to clearly segregate the areas used by employees from those dedicated to receiving visitors and the general public.

The main design element is a curved wall in the center of the floor plan, clearly separating the public and private areas, with the offices on one side and the meeting rooms and restrooms on the other. The wall has been designed so that it interrupts all the visual lines running from the entrance to the offices. According to Craig Downey, this element was inspired by the relief works of the painter Ben Nicholson. The designer has skillfully interpreted the function of the walls as a kind of limit or frontier in a clever interplay of doors, openings, and empty spaces.

A canvas of white cotton hangs from the upper part of the wall. This is an element that Downie has used previously (specifically, in his Job Center in Southall), and whose use here is due to its undeniable advantages over a traditional plaster ceiling: easy removal for repairs and its tendency to diffuse light. Other similarities between this design and the Southall project include the furnishings, the finishes, and the color scheme.

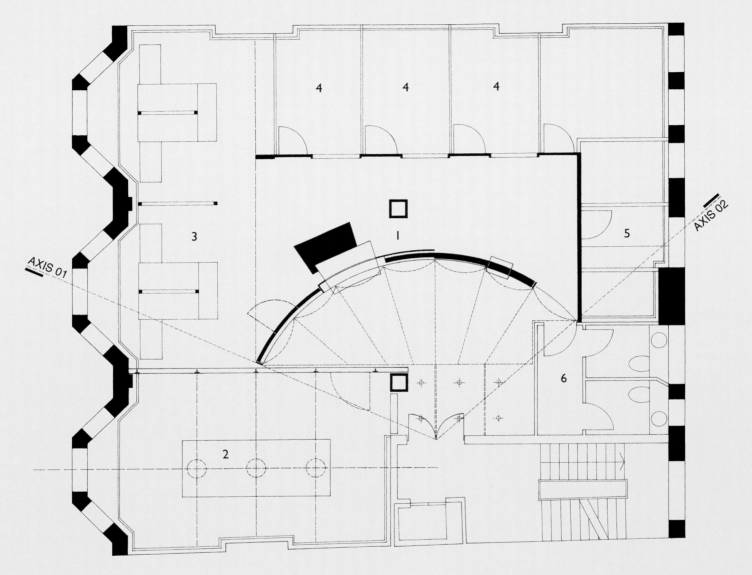

AXIS 01

AXIS 02

Floor plan.

1. Reception.
2. Meeting and conference
   room.
3. Administration.
4. Offices.
5. Gallery.
6. Washrooms.

A glass wall with an adjustable, laminated
curtain separates the reception area
from the meeting rooms.

The surface area is quite small and yet
the architects of the Downey Studio have
been able to create an interesting and
complex space in which the differences
between the various environments
have been perfectly defined.

CDC Investment Management, Ltd.

Location: *Piccadilly, London.*
Inauguration date: *1998.*
Client: *EIML, Caisse de Dépôts.*
Design: *Studio Downie Architects (Craig Downie, Andrew Jackson, Laura Downie).*
Associates: *Davis Langdon & Everest (Quantity Surveyors).*
Photography: *Peter Cook.*

109

Atelier CANAL *Avant la Lettre*

The last remaining printing works in the city of Paris were removed in 1993 to be transformed into new 55,700-square-foot, 1,000-employee offices for the publishing firm of Bayard Presse. Daniel and Patrick Rubin, two members of Atelier CANAL, had to remodel a ground floor with a complex perimeter, so complex, in fact, that it was actually the sum of five different buildings. The architects decided to endow the offices with an intelligible order and, as far as possible, to let natural light into the interior through minor operations carried out on the antiquated structural system.

The project is structured around an urbanistic network: the construction of a series of streets leading into plazas, each with a specific function (hall, employee break room, meeting point, file room), provides identity to what otherwise would simply be a spatial sequence. In addition to this, the architects have managed to admit natural light in certain strategic spaces, such as the file room. The opening of a double space and the existence of an inner patio make it possible to illuminate the library through a large skylight.

On one of the inner streets a link has been established between the ground floor and the second floor, where the editorial staff of the newspaper La Croix have their offices. In this way, illumination from above is obtained, as well as an interesting visual relationship between two sections of the same company. A walkway with a glass ceiling connects all the meeting rooms. Finally, most of the walls have polished, reflecting surfaces that duplicate the effects of the light.

*Daniel and Patrick Rubin
use glass to create
reflections and
transparencies that
multiply the light and
enrich the spaces.*

ELEVATION RUE BAYARD

Longitudinal section.

*The use of color
superimposes a subliminal
network of references on
the geometry.*

General ground plan

1. Entry.
2. Reception.
3. Library.
4. General amenities.

5. Dispatch zone.
6. Post room.
7. Inner street.
8. File room.
9. Meeting point.

10. Lavatories.
11. Kitchen.
12. Break room.
13. Meeting rooms.
14. Gallery.

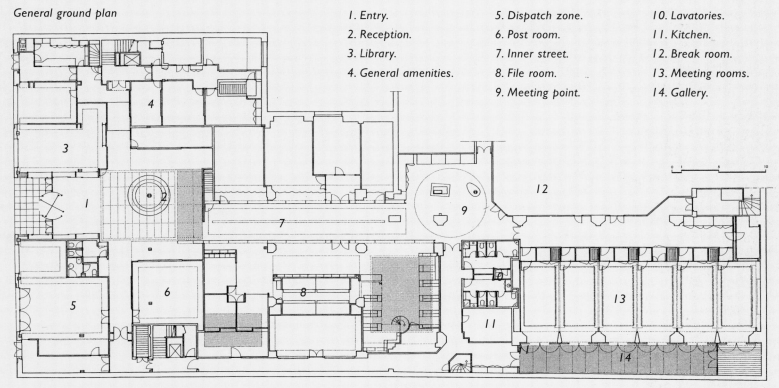

PLAN REZ-DE-CHAUSSEE

At the far end of the
building there are six large,
adjacent meeting rooms,
connected by a gallery with
a large skylight. Inside are
the strikingly colored Arne
Jacobsen-designed chairs.

View of the reception area. The
artist Gatimalau contributed
to the ceiling design.

The structure of the old industrial buildings that contained the printing presses has been cleaned and left bare, establishing a contrast with the new materials.

Atelier CANAL

Atelier CANAL are the architects Daniel Rubin, Patrick Rubin and Eric Puzenat.

Main works between 1990-1998: Libération newspaper offices, Paris; Museums of France Department offices, Paris; Maison du Livre, Chaumont; 200 student apartments in Annecy; renovation of the National Theater of Strasbourg; Paribas Bank head offices; Club Méditerranée head offices.

Bayard Presse

Address: *3-5, Rue Bayard, Paris, France.*
Completion date: *1995.*
Client: *Bayard Presse.*
Cost: *15,500,000 francs.*
Project: *Atelier CANAL, consisting of Daniel Rubin, Patrick Rubin.*
Collaborators: *Eric Puzenat (assistant); Terrell Rooke Associés (structure); Noble Ingenierie (fluids); Gatimalau (guest artist); SOPAC (contractor); Silvera (furniture).*
Photographs: *Hervé Abbadie.*

Octavio Mestre Arquitectos Asociados

Conspiring with the Past

The project consisted of the refurbishment as offices of three adjacent buildings from different periods and in different styles: a small classic palace with a rear patio from the turn of the century, a mimetic extension of the same carried out in the 1950s, and an adjacent office block from the 1970s, the latter of no architectural interest whatsoever.

Octavio Mestre's idea was to preserve and heighten the unique character of the palace in dense surroundings of high-rise buildings. To that end, the moldings, coffered ceilings, curved marquetry doors and original cornices have all been restored. At the same time, specific operations were carried out such as the transformation of the coach entry into the main door to the offices and the construction of a pergola on one of the front facade balconies.

The extension built in the 1950s has been totally transformed by opening an interior patio and building a new stair nucleus. The facade of the adjacent building has been renovated with the superimposition of a metal skin and large slatted windows. The new facade gives priority to the access patio in relation to contact with the street, which is very narrow. For the interior finishes, Octavio Mestre sought contrast between the warm tones of wood and the bluish reflections of sheet metal. He used glass for transparency and used polished, reflecting surfaces to mitigate the light.

Detail of the palace entry. The reception desk was designed by Octavio Mestre.

Ground floor.

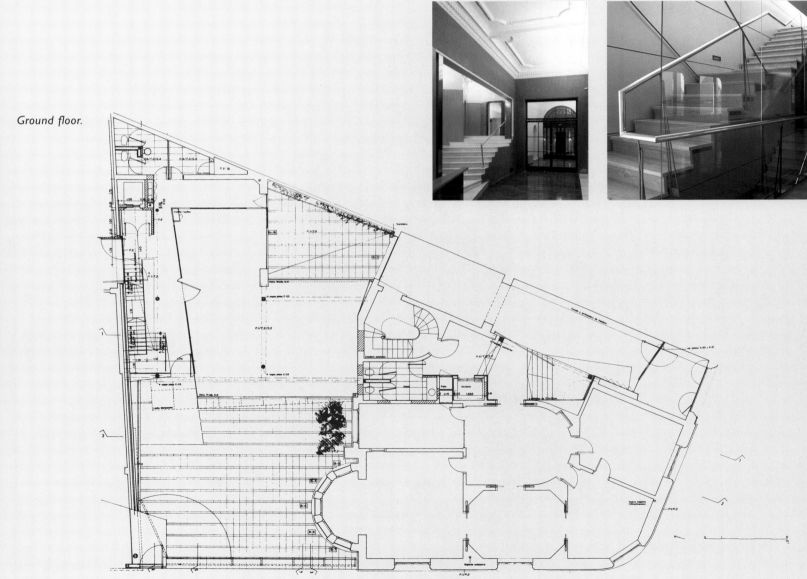

Attic.

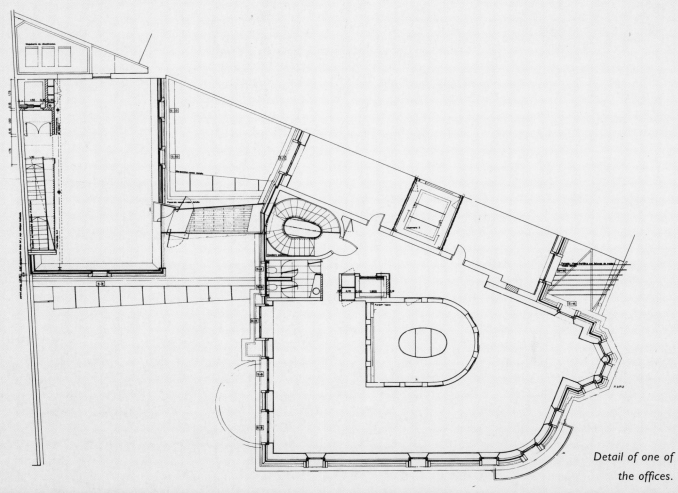

*Detail of one of
the offices.*

Octavio Mestre

1960. Born in Lleida, Spain
1985. Graduates as an architect
from the ETSA (Escola Tècnica
Superior d'Arquitectura), Barcelona.
1987-1990. Barcelona municipal
architect.
1991. Founds Octavio Mestre
Arquitectos Asociados.

Main recent works: Apartment
block in El Putxet, Barcelona; Casa
Bachero, Cubelles; Restaurante Le
Mex, Barcelona; Prosegur Head
Office, L'Hospitalet; Torre Mapfre
Offices, Barcelona; refurbishment of
Muebles Tarragona, Barcelona; Virgin
Megastore, Barcelona; 27 houses in
Toulouse

Offices on Diagonal and Minerva

Address: *Av. Diagonal and
Minerva, Barcelona, Spain.*
Completion date: *1995.*
Client: *Europrado.*
Project: *Octavio Mestre.*
Collaborators: *Eudald Pérez, Shaun
Pilgrem, Xavier Valls, Pepe Vivas
(architects); Gabriel Cano (surveyor);
Robert Brufau (structural engineer);
Sulzer (heating and air-conditioning);
Simatec (electrical consultant); Secotec
(quality control); Construcciones y
Contratas (general contractor)*
Photographs: *Duccio Malagamba,
Octavio Mestre.*

Wortmann Bañares
Arquitectos | ***Wooden Computers***

With an area of 1,200 square feet, these offices house the nerve center of a futures firm that handles vast flows of electronic money whose physical existence is reduced to ephemeral figures on computer monitors. Unlike many of today's designers who seek to include images inspired from cyberspace, Bañares and Wortmann consider the presence of virtual reality as an object of reflection and not as something that should determine form.

Their idea in this case is to temper the incorporation of information technology in work spaces. While undeniable that new technologies have transformed our perception of reality, it is equally true that our links to specific kinds of spaces, furniture, and materials have not changed in the same way. Bañares and Wortmann prefer not to literally reproduce the aesthetics of computers in architecture; on the contrary, they strive to introduce it more subtly and less directly.

As a result, the flashing images on screens suggest the incorporation of polished surfaces and translucent glass that cause reflections and transparencies, like an extension of the traditional office. Even so, and despite the importance of technology for this firm, the atmosphere of its offices is surprisingly homelike and relaxing. In this sense, the project does not fall into the trap of virtuality; rather it goes back to what is truly important: the feeling of comfort and empathy with space on the part of the company employees.

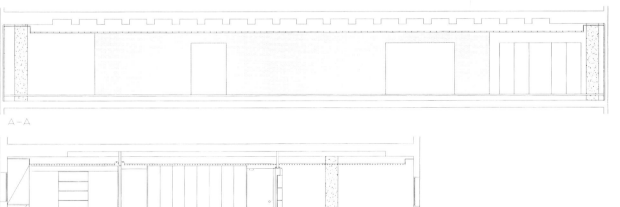

A-A

B-B

Cross section.
Longitudinal section.

The plaster has been
removed from the
pillars, leaving the
bare concrete to
contrast with the
other materials.

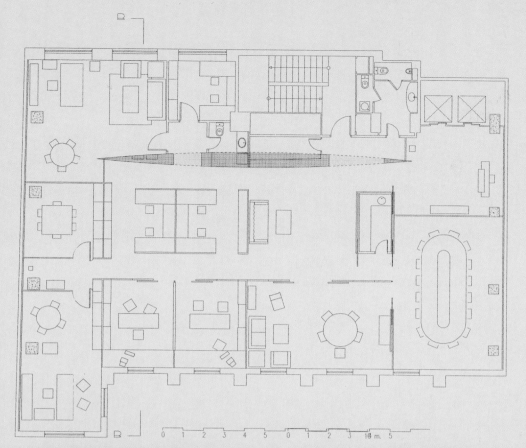

General ground plan.

The offices are housed in a turn-of-the-century building that admits very little natural light. Through the use of translucent glass as partitions and metal surfaces, the architects have striven to take maximum advantage of the little light available

Guillermo Bañares

1951. Born in Barcelona, Spain. Graduated as architect from ETSA, Barcelona.
1984. Sets up his own practice.

Johannes Wortmann

1955. Born in Soest, Germany. Graduates as architect from the Technical University of Berlin.
1989. Joins Bañares' practice.

Main recent works: Casa García-Hoz, Madrid; Casa Torrents, Puigcerdà; Casa Llongueras, Esplugues; contracts room of Global Securities, Barcelona; Coopers & Lybrand head office, Barcelona; GGK offices, Barcelona.

MEFF

Address: *Vía Layetana 58, Barcelona, Spain.*
Completion date: *1996.*
Client: *MEFF Project: Guillermo Bañares, Johannes K. Wortmann*
Collaborators: *David Regales (furniture); M & S (project management).*
Photographs: *Lluís Casals.*

Rowing Against the Current

Wortmann Bañares Arquitectos

Guillermo Bañares and Johannes Wortmann have striven to offset the hierarchical symmetry, compactness and technological pragmatism of the headquarters of Recoletos Publishers in Barcelona with other strategies and interpretations that, while thoroughly respectful of the original concept, enrich a work environment that would otherwise be excessively unidirectional. The headquarters is in a recently built office block with curtain-wall facades, impeccable finishes, large distances between pillars (23 by 33 feet), an almost symmetrical ground plan, raised floors so that installations can pass beneath, and false ceilings.

The building itself has already met a considerable number of needs and establishes a strong precedent from which it is highly difficult to deviate. All that was left to do was choose from among a great variety of partitions and office furniture designs available on the market. Instead of creating compartments through the use of partitions, Wortmann and Bañares have created a more fluid space in which the separation between different work areas is established by shelves and cupboards.

These separations result in several levels of transparency, and give workers a variety of possible routes to follow through the building. Similarly, the architects have introduced materials not commonly found in offices, such as fiber-cement, and chosen furniture that readily reveals the passing of time. If the project seems dissonant in some respects, as in the case of the excessively uniform false ceiling of plaster plaques, this may paradoxically be because the original building had already been too complete.

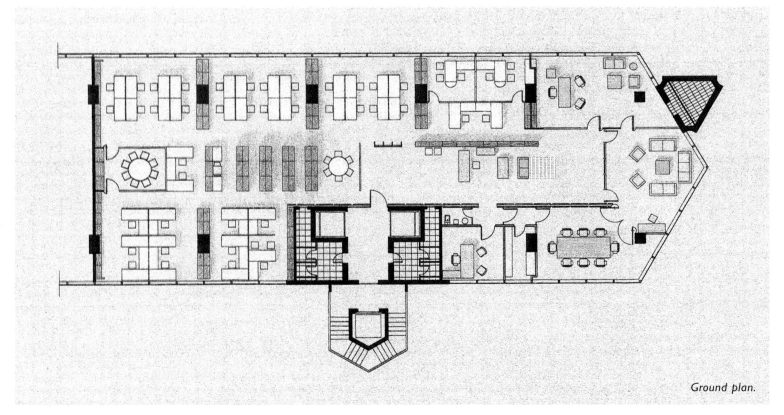

Ground plan.

Detail of one of the fiber-
cement walls. In the
foreground, one of the
series of cardboard chairs
designed by Frank O.
Gehry.

Recoletos Publishers

Address: *Diagonal 640, Barcelona,
Spain.*
Completion date: *1995.*
Client: *Recoletos Publishers.*
Project: *Guillermo Bañares and
Johannes K. Wortmann.*
Collaborator: *David Regales
(furniture).*
Photographs: *Joan Mundó.*

Sevil Peach Gence Associates *Reflections on the 15th Floor*

Sony Europe Finance was one of the first companies to occupy space in the renovated Commercial Tower Union building after damage caused by a terrorist bomb had been repaired. Sony executives had the privilege of choosing the 15th floor, and consequently, their offices enjoy spectacular views of Lloyds Tower, a landmark in high-tech architecture, and of Southwest London from Tower Bridge to St Paul's Cathedral.

With their total area of approximately 3,280 square feet, the offices include large work areas as well as private offices and conference rooms. The aim of Sevil Peach Gence Associates was to minimize the impact of their intervention on the building's structure, considered by many to be the finest high-rise in London. Their strategy consisted of developing a system of partitions separated from the facade by glass panels. In this way, they achieved a twofold effect. On one hand the partitions are invisible from the exterior, and thus the appearance of the building is respected; on the other hand, the view of the city from each of the offices is considerably extended, since the lateral glass panels make it possible to open oblique visual lines.

The building's ground plan is an exact square. The central part is occupied by stairwells and elevator shafts, services, and installation galleries, so that the space devoted exclusively to offices is a perimetric strip. Sevil Peach Gence Associates have described two rings: a corridor that also contains the services and auxiliary rooms (kitchen, photocopy room, smokers' lounge, machine room, filing cabinets), and a wider strip that, on the east and west facades, has no partition, and on the north and south facades includes the directors' offices and conference rooms.

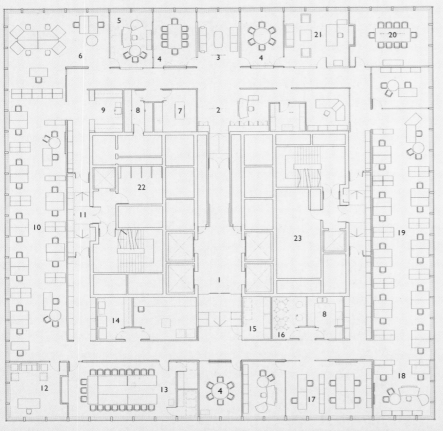

General plan.

1. Elevator hall.
2. Reception.
3. Waiting area.
4. Meeting room.
5. General manager's office.
6. Contracts.
7. Machine room.
8. Kitchen.
9. Post room.
10. Planning and accounting.
11. Fire escape.
12. Visitors' lounge.

13. Conference room.
14. Photocopy room.
15. Storeroom.
16. Smokers' lounge.
17. Projects area.
18. Executive office.
19. SCN Group.
20. Boardroom.
21. Director's office.
22. Ladies' toilet.
23. Gentlemen's toilet.

Detail of the central corridor. The use of glass and blue and gray tones predominate in the offices.

One of the meeting rooms.
All office furniture is by
Vitra and Coexistence.

Sevil Peach Gence

1949. Born in Turkey and educated in Seattle.
1966. Graduates in interior design from the Brighton College of Art and Design, UK.
1977-1985. Works as an associate of Sir Frederick Gibberd & Partners.
1985. Founds her own studio.

Main recent works: Barclays Bank, London; National Bank of Uzbekistan, Uzbekistan; Standard Chartered Bank, Hong Kong; AR Hotel, Chicago; Gatwick Sterling Hotel, London; Aygaz Limited, Istanbul; private hospital in Brunei.

Sony Europe Finance

Location: *Commercial Union Tower, London, UK.*
Completion date: *1995 (1st phase), 1997 (2nd phase).*
Client: *Sony United Kingdom Limited.*
Project: *Sevil Peach Gence Associates.*
Collaborators: *Palmer Associates (executive architects); Hilson Moran Partnership (installations consultants); Walter Lilly & Co., Churchfield Associates (builders, 1st and 2nd phases); Vitra and Coexistence (furniture); Erco (lighting); Mannington (carpets).*
Photographs: *Dennis Gilbert/VIEW.*

Sir Norman Foster & Partners *Clean Technology*

The seven-story Business Promotion Center in Duisburg is the landmark building of the Park. The center is designed to regenerate business and promote growth in the Ruhr Region. It was the result of a particularly creative collaboration with Kaiser Bautechnik, the environmental engineers and pioneers of energy efficient building systems.

The ground floor contains a banking and exhibition hall in a double-height space. Office and conference spaces occupy the remaining area culminating in a grand three-story internal terrace, which can be leased commercially. The building is equipped with highly advanced technological systems both for energy efficiency and comfort control. Two types of solar cell will be installed on the roof to subsidize the energy required by the gas-powered cogenerator, the principal power source for the building. Photovoltaic cells harness solar energy to feed into the electricity supply. Solar panels heat water, which is then fed to an absorption cooler to chill water for the radiant cooling system.

This integrated approach to energy creation allows the building owner to make a profit on the energy sold to tenants. The internal environment is maintained by separate heating and air-conditioning systems. Chilled water passes through a system of pipes encased in metal conductors concealed within a suspended ceiling, which then cools the air in the internal spaces. Fresh air is fed through channels at floor level and creates a low level lake of air that gradually rises as it warms up. The reduced cross-sectional area required for ducts minimizes the floor-to-floor height and, therefore, the cost of the building was reduced compared to a normal air-conditioned office.

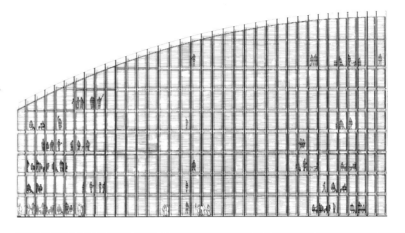

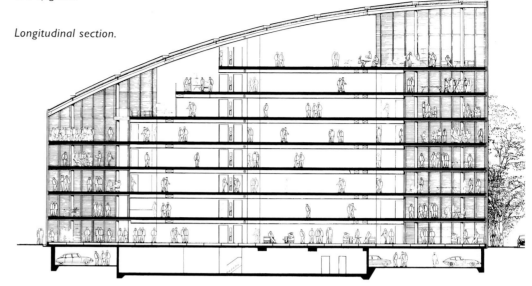

View of the three-level interior terrace. The handrails and doors are of glass.

Longitudinal section.

View of the meeting room. The facade features a sophisticated computer-controlled blinds system.

Typical floor. Forms and the sharp slope of the roof create strange visual effects and false perspectives.

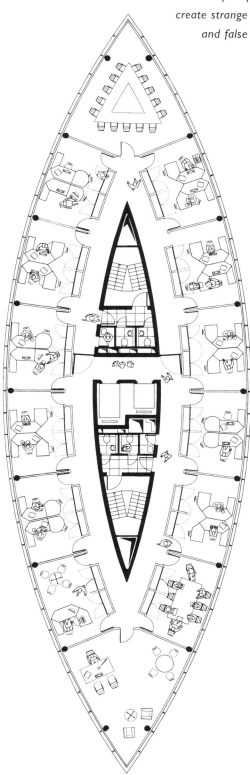

Inside the white walls and ceilings combine with the soft gray of the carpet. The chair upholstery, the table tops and the rest of the furniture are all in variations of gray. It seems as if color has been excluded as something alien to work spaces.

Sir Norman Foster

1935. Born in Manchester (UK).
1961. Graduates as an architect from Manchester University.
1967. Founds Foster Associates with Wendy Foster.
1968-1983. Collaborates with Buckminster Fuller on several projects. **1967-1990.** Hong Kong and Shanghai Bank offices in Hong Kong.
1990. Founds Sir Norman Foster & Partners.

Recent works (1990-1998):
Stansted Airport; Century Tower, Tokyo; Carré d'Arts, Nîmes; Cranfield University Library; Law Faculty, Cambridge; Joselyn Art Museum, Nebraska.

Business Promotion Center

Location: *Duisburg Germany.*
Completion Date: *1994.*
Client: *Business Promotion Center and Telematic Center.*
Project: *Sir Norman Foster & Partners.*
Collaborators: *Reinhold Meyer (structural engineer); Kaiser Bautechnik (project controller); J. Roger Preston & Partners, Rud Otto Meyer, Kaiser Bautechnik (electrical/mechanical engineer).*
Photographs: *Architekturphoto.*

Jonas

Erick van Egeraat | *Inside the Whale*

On entering a fin-de-siècle building in Vienna or Budapest, one is swept away by magical realism as if in a story by Kafka. It was this same impression that hit Erick van Egeraat as he opened the door into this building in the business district of the Hungarian capital. Over a hundred years old, the house features a facade combining classicism, the Baroque, and Art Nouveau.

The project entailed converting an 1880 residential building into the Budapest office of Nationale Nederlanden Hungary and ING Bank. Erick van Egeraat judged that this process of restoration-cum-conversion should include something absolutely new, as a contrast to the antique atmosphere of the building. Consequently, the hall is an independent element leading the visitor on a journey through time from the end of the 19th century to the present day.

Unseen from the street, a large whale-shaped dome emerges from the ceiling. The details of the glass roof and the "whale" are at the same time explicit and extreme, in order to match the rest of the design details. The laminated glass beams, 16 inches wide with a span of 11 feet 6 inches, support a transparent glass curtain where the vast marine mammal floats. The stainless steel joints between the glass support structure and the main structure are covered with hinged bars. Throughout the main structure, each of the 483 pieces that swim in the sea of glass has a different form.

Section.

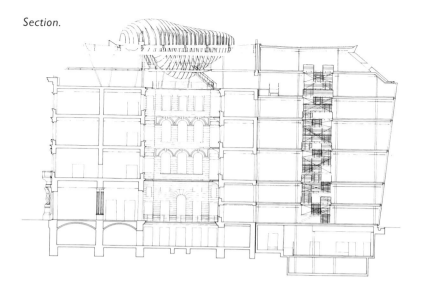

Ground floor.

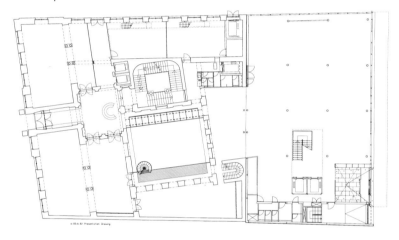

Attic.

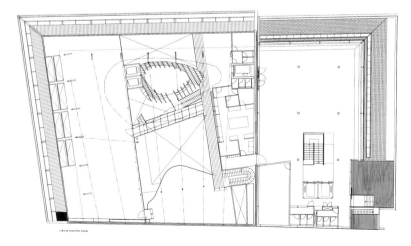

View of the café corner structure.

Sketch of the whale, in which can be seen the origins of the concept for the roof.

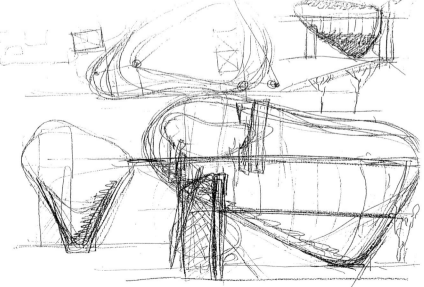

Erick van Egeraat

1956. Born in Amsterdam.
1983. Co-founder of MECANOO
Architects.
1984. Graduates from the Technical
University of Delft.
1995. Founds EEA, Erick van Egeraat
Associated Architects.

Main recent works: Housing in Park
Haagseweg, Amsterdam; Public Library
in Almelo; Economics Faculty, Utrecht;
Natural History Museum, Rotterdam.

ING Bank

Address: *Office Building Paulay Ede Utca
12, Budapest (Hungary).*
Completion date: *1995.*
Client: *Nationale Nederlanden Hungary,
Ltd., Budapest (J. Szamel); ING Bank,
Budapest (Tibor E. Rejto); ING Real Estate,
The Hague (P. Koch, Jan Everts).*
Architect: *Erick van Egeraat.*
Collaborators: *ABT Adviesburo voor
Bouwtechniek b.v., Delft (structures); Ketel
Raadgevend Ingenieurs d.v., Delft
(mechanical and electric services);
Permasteelisa, Conegliano (glass
construction); Henk Bouwer, Avi Lev, Delft
(maquettes).*
Photographs: *Christian Richters.*

Nikken Sekkei | *The Opulent Void*

This 20-story building, head office of the Long-Term Credit Bank of Japan, is in the center of Tokyo next to Hibiya Park. The T-shaped structure allows the base of the tower to be narrower than the rest of the building, making possible a small square opposite the facade. Part of the square is occupied by two huge 98-foot-high glass boxes, each containing an entrance foyer to the offices.

The T-shape is both a technical feat (a computer-controlled system prevents the cantilever from swaying) and a demonstration of power. Indeed, all the public rooms (foyer, conference room, receptions room, cafeteria, and break room) have a spectacular, representative character. In a nation accustomed to small interiors and in a city where the price of land is exorbitant, this building blatantly squanders space. In this sense, the top floor is the most representative.

The two ends of the building, with splendid panoramic views over the city of Tokyo, are occupied by a 40-foot high conference room and a room in which to receive visitors. Its proportions are reminiscent more of an opera auditorium than a work space. Through the huge windows the city's high-rises appear dwarfed. The rooms are practically empty except for a few easy chairs, a table, and a rug. Scales are transformed on the 20th floor: the slightest architectural gesture feels as though it carries more weight than the rest of the world.

Several views of the
entrance foyer.

Detail of one of the conference rooms.

Employees' break room on the 8th floor.

Plan of the bottom part of the tower.

Plan of the top part of the tower.

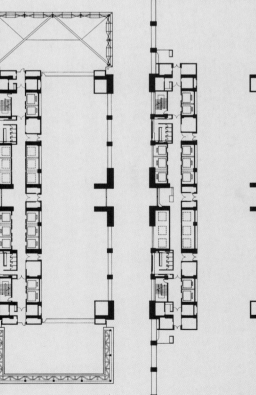

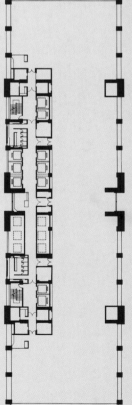

Room in which to receive visitors.

Nikken Sekkei

1900. Nikken Sekkei, Ltd., is founded in Tokyo. With its three head offices in Tokyo, Osaka, and Nagoya, Nikken Sekkei is a firm of consultants that draws up architectural projects and landscape designs and supervises urban projects and services all over the world. Throughout its history, the company has participated in over 13,000 projects, both public and private, in 40 countries. It employs over 2,000 specialists in Japan, thus constituting one of the largest firms of its kind in the world. Apart from another 10 offices in Japan, it has offices in Seoul, Kuala Lumpur, and Shanghai, and is affiliated with major consultants all over the world.

Recent projects: Osaka World Trade Center, Osaka; Bunyo Civic Center, Tokyo; Solid Square, Tokyo.

Long-Term Credit Bank of Japan

Location: *Chiyota Ward, Tokyo, Japan.*
Completion date: *1994.*
Client: *Long-Term Credit Bank of Japan.*
Project: *Nikken Sekkei.*
Collaborators: *Takenaka Corporation (general contractor).*
Photographs: *Nacasa & Partners.*